CREATING YOUR CLASSIC CAREER

ALISON SPENCER

Published in 2016 by Fight or Flight Publishing

ISBN Paperback: 978-0-9935381-0-0
ebook: 978-0-9935381-1-7

A catalogue record of this book is available from the British Library and the National Library of Scotland)

Published with the help of

IndieAuthors
World

Dedication

For Graham, Kara and Ross. Loved always.

Acknowledgements

I couldn't have written this on my own. I'd like to thank everyone who took time out of their busy schedules to assist me in my research. Sharing of knowledge is a powerful tool; without it we would remain stagnant in our lives. To Leila Khan at Life is Today Academy for subconsciously giving me the idea in the first place. To Kim and Sinclair MacLeod at Indie Authors World for making my dream of becoming a published author a reality. To Shirley Waddell with assisting with research, Fiona Prior for editing and proofreading and Amanda Bennie for her fantastic HR input and her constructive feedback, along with Moraig Hewitt, Mags Corr and Graham Spencer for giving me different perspectives on careers.

Alison

Creating your Classic Career

Chapter 1

Introductions

Do you ever imagine how it would feel to wake up every morning blessed because you are going to the job you love? Do you ever wonder how you would feel to face Monday mornings with a smile on your face and banish the Sunday night blues? Well, now you can!

I secured my first job in 1994, and it has taken me until now to realise that finding your perfect job is not outwith your reach. Okay, it is by no means plain sailing. It requires dedication, commitment and a lot of self-awareness to fulfil your dreams. In this book I am going to share with you various techniques and tips to help you on your journey.

What qualifies me to write this book? Well, I don't have any qualifications on paper. But what I possess is real life experience. I've been there, standing in your shoes. I know the frustrations you face and the barriers you hit. I know what it's like to feel miserable in the daily grind, thinking I would never escape. But I also know that you will come out the other side stronger, with a new determination to succeed.

I first started out working in recruitment, and then spent a further 15 years in the financial sector, carrying out administrative and business support. Don't get me wrong, I loved the people and the company was generous to its employees; we always received a bonus at Christmas, and a good lifestyle/work was also promoted. It looked perfect on paper. But I was bored. This wasn't a career, it was a job. And I felt that if I continued with it until retirement I would go mad!

So, in 2011 I decided to set up my own business, working in conjunction with my 'day job' until I built up a client base. I provided administration support and writing services to clients, predominantly CV writing. In 2014 I gave up my 'real job' to be a full-time self-employee.

But I knew my business was not going the way I wanted it. Preparing CVs and mentoring people on career paths were my passion. So, along with my life coach, Leila Khan, I changed my business model, concentrating more on career aspects rather than administration support. I had gained various experiences in a voluntary capacity, including mentoring young people on CV writing and interview techniques. I knew I was good at writing CVs; I gained a lot of positive feedback from clients. I now work as a Career Development Consultant, providing all aspects of career coaching including CV writing skills, interview techniques and presentation coaching. I've also worked with various charities including Deafblind Scotland and Shelter, and Volunteer Tutors Organisation.

Statistically, we spend more time at our jobs than we do with our friends and family. Scary, isn't it? That's why we owe it to ourselves to create our very own classic career. I hope you learn something positive from my shared knowledge and experiences. Happy reading, I hope you enjoy it.

Alison Spencer, The Write Career, 2015

Chapter 2

Career planning

2.1 Mind maps and their usefulness

As you will see as you progress throughout this book, I am a huge fan of mind maps and flowcharts. Mind maps help you through a designated process using diagrams to visually structure information. They have been around for a very long time, as early as the third century BC. They can provide clarity to all those muddling thoughts draining your energy. By using pictures and processes instead of solely using listening and audio skills I can see at a glance what my options are, and the different paths I can take to reach my goal.

There are no set rules in how to design a mind map. While the most popular method is to start in the centre and draw outwards, I like starting at the left hand side of a page and go round in a full circle. It really doesn't matter, as long as it makes sense to you.

Mind maps are also useful in providing insight to others. Imagine being lucky enough to decide what your classic career will be. But your classic career means revisiting your lifestyle and making major changes to your life. You are so excited and apprehensive, you immediately tell your spouse/partner/family, 'I'm going to be a teacher, and I'm going to leave my secure, well-paying job and go back to university!' What would their likely reactions be? Would they be pleased? Or angry that you hadn't discussed this with them first? Would they see this as just a whim because you had a bad day at the office? It could be any one of these scenarios, you just don't know. Instead of sitting down and pouring out your decisions and dreams in one hasty breath, it would be much easier to have a logical plan already drawn out before you discuss it with others, that includes all your thought processes and options. That way, they will see that you have really thought about it and it's not just something you thought up five minutes beforehand.

Mind maps are not set in stone. They are also a useful reference to have. If you have decided to go down one path and it is not working, refer back to your mind map. What could you do to change paths? What are the other options available to you? By already having a strategy in place, it will be a lot easier to see where else you can change your route. It is amazing to look back and see how you achieved your goal. Nine times out of ten, the path we take is not the original we mapped out for ourselves, which is evident from the case studies at the end of this book.

2.2 Why?

Why, indeed! Why is a career so important? Some would name money in the first instance. Without a job we have no money. Without money we cannot purchase the basics like food and drink. We cannot pay our bills. And we may lose social contact, with no finances left to enjoy our hobbies or go out for a meal with friends. But I am talking about a career, not a job. These two things are very different. Let me explain.

A job

When we first venture into the world of work, the majority of us are looking for a job (as explained above) to make money, which is our short-term goal. Whether it be a paper round when we are still at school, or a weekend job in a shop; we work to buy the latest fashions, go out with friends or go on holiday. We don't want – or need – to build a career at this stage. This could be a continuous pattern, some people work in the same job throughout their working lives. There is nothing wrong with this if they are happy, and earn money to keep their standard of living level throughout.

A career

A career builds on more long-term goals. It may be as early as graduating from university. Or, like me, it can happen in later life. I've always thought it was impossible for students to be expected to know exactly what they want to do when they leave school. It was the same for me. I hadn't gained any life experience, except for working in my local supermarket, and, as described above, this was for my own short-term goals; to have enough spending money for ice skating on Saturday nights with friends, lipstick and magazines.

When I talk about goals in this book, I am referring to SMART goals (Specific, Measurable, Achievable, Realistic, Time-bound), not unrealistic dreams. There is no point telling yourself that you want to be a famous rock star when you can't sing! Chasing goals and dreams that are realistically unobtainable will have a huge detrimental impact on your well-being.

SMART goals summarise your performance expectations in a practical, methodical and strategic manner. Think of a goal you want to achieve, then write down the steps using the SMART diagram below:

SPECIFIC
How will I reach this goal?
Who/What/Where/Why/When?

MEASURABLE
Track and measure progress, use milestones to reach small achievements on your way
Know when the goal has been met

ATTAINABLE
Is the task feasible?
How much commitment do I need?
What additional resources do I need?

SMART

TIME-BOUND
Ensure there is enough time to achieve the goal
What are the start and end dates?

REALISTIC
Am I willing and able to reach this goal?
Are sufficient resources available?

I've given a short scenario to help you:

Kate is a secretary within a large corporate organisation. She has been there for five years. She would now like to move into the training side, and has been thinking of this for a while. Kate does not want to talk to her manager about this before she has set out her goals as back up. Below is how Kate has summarised her goals using the SMART method:

Specific – Having undergone a personal and professional development course I have now decided I want to move from the secretarial support team to become a training and development coach for client-facing teams.

Measurable – I am going to go on a six month training programme starting in the next two months, arrange for work shadowing, undertake qualifications, and set interim dates to meet with my line manager to discuss my progression.

Attainable – Through discussion with my training department I have found a position due to expansion in autumn 2016 for which I plan to apply. I will talk to my manager first about my goal, then I will arrange cover for my role before I go on the training programme.

Realistic – I want to achieve this goal as I love teaching others to help them be the best that they can be within their role which in turn will lead to a more productive and enthusiastic workforce and will help establish me as an expert, along with my qualifications and training.

Time-bound – Within one year I will be fully qualified to undertake this role.

Careers are about developing your existing skills and learning new talents to move into the area you want to work in, and keep progressing in. You have a passion for what you do and are keen to keep training and learning to move up the career ladder.

So, careers are important to us because they give us a sense of accomplishment. Imagine you are on your way home after a busy day; your feet hurt, your head aches and you feel exhausted. But you feel elated because you achieved something. That's what the classic career can bring. The mind map below shows evidence of this. If you feel a sense of accomplishment, you feel good about yourself. That will in turn generate positive feelings and you will also feel happy in your home life.

Please bear in mind that your feelings of exhaustion should be short-term. If you are leaving work every day feeling this way, be careful not to burn out. Your career should still allow you a decent work/lifestyle balance. We all need time off to recharge our batteries.

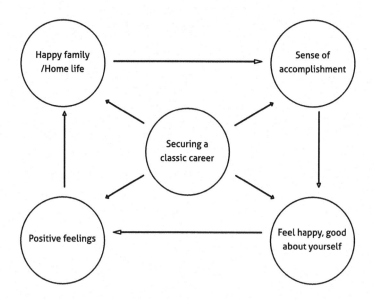

2.3 What?

What is a decision only you can make, but you can seek a little help along the way. If, for example, you've been in a job, or indeed, a career, for a long period of time, you may think it is time for a change and you may wish to move into a completely different industry. But what? It's not just school leavers that find difficulty in making career decisions.

The first thing to do is to make a list. What interests you? What are your key strengths? Would you have to go back to studying for your dream role? Can you work part-time in your old job to keep the money coming in? All these decisions are important ones to make, and should not be taken lightly. If you are really struggling, I would highly recommend a life coach to help you on the right path. Contact details can be found at the end of this book.

But what can a life coach help you to achieve? Leila Khan, of Life is Today Academy, explains: *'Life is today, right here, right now, this is the only moment that exists and it's only in this moment that we can create the future that we dream of; the abundance mindsets, the goals, the life-changing decisions and living in the moment. The power of a question should never be underestimated as, through skilful questioning during coaching, you can experience powerful personal transformation, toward your dream goals and desires.'*

2.4 How?

Once you have decided what you want to achieve, the next step is to decide how you are going to achieve it. This depends on a number of factors:

1. **How will I find ways to invest? (financial and time period)**

2. **How committed am I?**

3. **End result**

It could be as simple as changing company/roles to a more senior position in your chosen field. Or it could be a complete change of career. This is when more thought is needed in the 'How' process. If you are already in the right career, but you want to move up the career ladder, your thought process will be simplified. Yes, you will still have to work hard to achieve that promotion, and you will still have to invest time into your next challenge, but monetary investment will be minimal. If you decide to have a complete change, this could be timely and costly, and may take a while to reach your end result. This is where you need to implement patience and visualise the end goal.

You now need to refer to your list you made in section 2.3. By now you should have hopefully worked out what working towards your classic career will entail, and what you need to do to put this into progress. The next step is to design a mind map showing logical steps of what you want and how you are going to achieve it:

What and How? Mind map

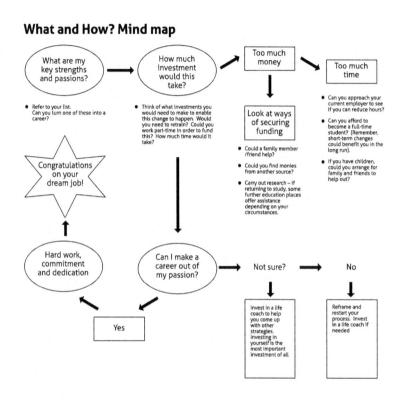

Chapter 3
Preparing your career writing tools

3.1 Curriculum Vitae

So you've created your mind map, worked out what you want to achieve, and how you are going to achieve it. You now have to sell your skills to a potential employer if you are looking for a career transformation, or a potential further education establishment if you need to undertake additional study.

Preparing a CV or application form is the most critical part of the career process. Without this document you cannot gain employment. With at least 50+ applications made to any one position, ensuring you are a step ahead of your competitors is crucial. You need to be able to outline your skills and achievements in a vibrant, concise and succinct way.

There are no set rules for a CV layout. If you have a look online templates differ. What I am going to share with you now is what I believe is the best way to lay out a CV that will hook a prospective employer and will secure you an interview. I've had a lot of success with clients who have prepared their CVs in this manner; one even secured an interview within two hours of him submitting his CV and was successful in obtaining that position. One client gained five interviews which subsequently led him to gain three job offers. You only have to look at this evidence to see that this format of CV really does get results – and fast. Take a look at my website for more testimonials. Details are at the end of the book.

I like to break a CV down into four separate parts:

1. Personal Statement/Profile section

The Personal Statement or Profile section at the beginning of the CV should state what you have done in the past, what you want to do next and the skills that connect the two. It should sum up the whole document and explain to the reader why your application is relevant to them. Keep it simple and specific. Mention the industries you have worked in, even some of the companies if they are well-known. Think along the lines of: What do *I* have to offer? What makes *me* stand out? Why is *my* application relevant to this job?

Remember to always tailor your profile to each individual job specification. If you have a lot of skills in various industries, emphasise the ones relevant to the job you are applying for. But don't just copy and paste sections out of the job specification. This looks unprofessional, and shows that you can't be bothered. Employers will notice!

For example, you could start along the lines of, 'A confident, versatile and enthusiastic customer service assistant, with 11 years' experience working in a retail environment, including shops such as Next, River Island, and Marks & Spencer'. These companies are recognised brands, so are worth mentioning if you have worked there.

Alternatively, if you have had experience in a local shop, you could say, 'A confident, versatile and enthusiastic customer service assistant, with 11 years' experience working in a local retail environment.'

Then go on to mention what you are looking for now. An example could be 'Now looking for a senior role within a similar remit.' Or, if you are looking for a complete change, 'Now looking to move into a hospitality environment.'

After this, you could mention what skills you have to offer, for example, 'Acknowledged as a focused and committed manager/team leader/individual, with the ability to motivate teams towards the successful delivery of a project within timescale and budget. Possesses strong communication and problem solving skills, liaising with appropriate personnel to achieve successful outcomes.'

How long should your profile be? There is a lot of conflicting advice on this. My advice is no longer than 10 lines. I know it is tempting to include everything, but you are not writing a novel. You need to learn how to dissect the important points from the waffle. A profile should hook the reader, making them want to find out more about you. You can expand your knowledge in the next section, Key Skills, Knowledge and Expertise.

I also like to write the Profile in third person, but this is a personal preference and there are no set rules for this.

Keywords and ATSs

Before we go any further looking at how to write and develop a CV, it is worth talking about keywords. As mentioned previously, it's not enough to have one generic CV for each job you apply for. Each CV needs to be tailored to each role, and employers will spot a generic CV a mile off.

Nowadays, some large companies use Applicant Tracking System (ATSs). These screening systems are introduced to cut the labour costs of manually reviewing the vast quantities of CVs submitted for each position. So, your CV may be rejected before a human eye has even looked at it if it is not tailored appropriately for the role you are applying for!

Keywords are therefore needed to strengthen your CV. Have a look in the job description to find them. Use the same keywords and phrases used in the job description, and repeat them as frequently as possible throughout your CV whilst remaining logical. This will give a better result within systems that use this software, and boost the chances of your CV being seen. These are effectively the same as SEO engines, however, don't just add in keywords without your CV making sense. So for example, if your CV stated you were a customer service assistant, and the particular job specification states 'customer service executive,' change the appropriate word in your CV to reflect this. Other examples include:

- Use specific nouns; instead of 'word processing' use 'Microsoft Word,' or 'MS Office.' Again, check the job description to see how the company words it. 'Work experience' may change to 'career or professional achievements.' Always check.

- Don't use any special fonts or characters. Use a standardise font such as Arial or Times New Roman.

- Spellcheck! An ATS will automatically reject spelling errors.

- Never send your CV in a pdf format. ATSs can misread these. A Word doc or docx file is best.

- Employment history section – ATSs look for names first. So list the name of the company, job title, and then date.

- Create a listed summary – list your achievements and skills, relevant to the job description. You can include buzzwords here, which will be discussed under Key Skills, Knowledge and Expertise.

Personally, I am not a fan of ATSs. Including specific words just for the sake of it is, in my opinion, not good practice and certainly not good writing. However, I can understand why companies have these. Sometimes, the rules have to broken to get a foot in the door!

2. Key Skills, Knowledge and Expertise

This section gives evidence of how you can apply and transfer your skills to various qualities through using specific sector/job title key words that employers are looking for.

Buzzwords are similar to keywords, and are used to make a CV stand out under Key Skills, Knowledge and Expertise. Employers want to be able to find if you demonstrate the essential criteria for the role on the first page of your CV.

These buzzwords can also help to strengthen your CV if ATSs are used.

Under this section, you can list your achievements and transferable skills along with evidence to back these up. Then write a short sentence of how you have used these skills within a career/life scenario.

Some examples of buzzwords and areas to include are:

- Teamwork (created, supported, guided, participated)

- Leadership (launched, managed, inspired, mentored, coached)

- Communication (presented, liaised, articulate)

- Problem solving (implemented, investigated, initiated)

- Negotiation (improved, quality, resilience)

- Customer service (focused, handling complaints, positive outcome, influenced)

- Dedication (conscientious, ethical, efficient).

These are not exhaustive. Check the job specification to see if any more are listed, and always tailor. Other areas to include could be language skills, awards, personal achievements (if relevant to application), IT/technical skills. For example, 'Company Salesperson of the Year 2013.' 'Engineering Associate Award 2014.'

However, as is the case with most things, people can become over-enthused and try to include every clichéd phrase possible. Words and phrases **NOT** to include are:

- Thinking outside the box

- Fun-loving

- Good sense of humour (it's not a dating advertisement! – see above point also)

- Paving the way to success

- Dynamic self-starter

- Cutting edge
- Reliable (so you can turn up on time, so what?)
- Go-getter
- Hard worker
- Expert
- Fully conversant with MS Office – this is a vague statement. You may be more advanced in one particular section of MS Office than the other. If you want to add this in, a way to do this would be:
  » 'IT Skills – MS Word (advanced), PowerPoint (intermediate), Excel (basic).'

It's argued that some keywords should not be included in a CV, for example, 'A team player.' 'Can work on own initiative.' Fair enough if this is all you write, but back it up with evidence in your career section. This could be reworded as 'guided and supported teams throughout a complex project, within budget.' 'Deputised for manager in his absence.' **Show** what you can do, instead of **tell.**

The points you list here may be used in competency-based questions should you get through to interview stage. Competency-based questions are questions whereby you are asked to provide real life examples and describe a situation where you demonstrated something in, like problem solving, using your initiative, or negotiating effectively. By putting pointers of these in your CV, the basis for these answers has already been provided.

3. Employment History

Now you need to follow this up with the Employment History section, which will provide evidence of how your key skills are put into practice.

For each of your jobs, include the company name and address, your job title and dates of employment. Start with the most recent job first. Then list your responsibilities in bullet point format, making it clear and concise.

Describe your employment history in terms of achievements. For each job, and particularly for your most recent roles, demonstrate what makes you stand out from other applicants. Remember to use the same or similar keywords and phrases from the advertisement – but don't copy sentences/plagiarise direct from job specification – again employers will notice!

Most of us have difficulty selling our skills. But you will be up against a lot of other applicants, so it is important to show exactly what the employer is looking for in a clear, concise manner, without overselling. Here are some pointers to note when you are thinking about your achievements:

- What have you done over and above your job description?

- Where have you gone beyond the extra mile?

- Where have you demonstrated flexibility, creative thinking or innovation?

- What projects have you been involved in and what was your contribution to the outcome?

- What problems did you solve?

Examples of these could be 'implemented a new filing system, which resulted in correspondence being found more quickly.' Or, 'worked late for a week to meet a project deadline which had been changed at short notice.' Or, 'devised a new stock system for the shop, resulting in reduced wastage.'

Also include facts and figures, the more specific detail you can include (and the less waffle) the better. For example:

- Costs, percentage improvements, key performance indicators met, targets met, costs saved, etc. 'Increased sales turnover by 42% against a target of 35%, which made us the highest performer out of seven teams' is much more effective than 'excellent sales management skills.'

It is important not to reveal confidential information in your application. If you are mentioning specific projects that are still ongoing, or have not been publicly announced, do not name any company/client names.

And remember to include voluntary work/internships/ placements. Just because you don't get paid for it doesn't mean it is not relevant.

So, as you can see, it doesn't have to be a long rambling statement, filled with numbers and big words. Use plain English and concise bullet points, backed up with examples and achievements of your roles and skills.

4. Education and Qualifications

The Education and Qualifications section can come before the Employment History or after, it really is a personal preference. I would advise, if you are a recent graduate or school leaver, to put this before the Employment History section as you may have more academic than employment experience. Include your most recent qualifications first, including any membership of professional bodies and **relevant** training courses. If you have gained a qualification a while ago, and it is no longer relevant, don't include it. Employers don't care if you gained your 'O' Grade/Level woodwork in 1985, if you are applying for a position as retail manager. Be sensible.

The exception to the rule

As with everything in life, there is always an exception to the rule. Sometimes you will need to deviate from chronological order so that you can highlight specific skills relevant to the role you are applying for. For example; you took a break from a sales role five years' ago to set up your own online retail business. You are now looking to move back into a similar sales-driven role as you realised being your own boss wasn't for you. You would then put your sales role **first**, under the heading 'Relevant Skills and Experience,' then list your other roles in chronological date order under 'Employment History.' That way, a potential employer will see you have the relevant skills from a first glance at your CV.

This is easier with application forms, as most of them ask to list your specific skills first, in the supporting statement section. We will look at application forms in section 3.3.

Gaps in employment history

Wouldn't it be great if life ran smoothly, we were successful in each job we applied for, and showed consistency throughout our employment history? Unfortunately, life rarely pans out like that. We all have unexpected gremlins that force us to make some crucial decisions that can ultimately affect our employment record. And that could mean your CV shows a gap in your employment history.

But this doesn't have to be a bad thing. Employers like honesty. So be authentic, but don't go into too much detail; some situations benefit from discretion. If you have career breaks in your employment history, it is best to mention them in your CV. Employers will notice these, so it is better to be upfront from the start. One common reason for a career break is to go travelling. But you need to expand on this. For example, you could say 'took a year out to go travelling, where I experienced living and working in multicultural environments.' Mention the work experience you did along the way, if any.

The same would apply if you took time out to raise a family, or became a carer for a family member. Mention this, most employers now like to encourage a work/lifestyle balance. For example, you could write, 'was primary carer to my father before his passing in [date],' or 'I raised my children, who are now in nursery/school aftercare and are no longer fully dependent on me.' You could also add in a little about how this gap influenced you, for example, 'this enhanced my organisational, planning and problem solving abilities, allowing me to multi-task within diverse environments.'

The tricky part is explaining leave of absence due to ill-health. This, again, can be put in a positive light, and doesn't have to hinder your chances. Instead of saying 'I was off sick with a recurring health problem for a year,' you could explain it as 'due to my recurring ill-health I felt it was of benefit to leave my last position. I have now fully recovered, am ready to re-enter the workforce and take on new challenges.'

If the gap wasn't your decision, explain it positively, and give examples of how this enabled you to refocus and become proactive to enhance your overall performance and dedication. Your cover letter can be used to enhance the gap if it was significant; don't go into too much detail in your CV, as this again will run the risk of it sounding like a novel.

You only have to explain gaps if these show discrepancies in your employment dates. If you were absent for a few weeks, or were on maternity/paternity leave and returned to the same workplace, these don't have to be disclosed.

What not to include in a CV

I've shown you previously what to include in a CV. Now I am going to talk about what not to include. As I keep mentioning, a CV should be concise. By eliminating these 'time wasters' space will be saved.

- 'CURRICULUM VITAE' – don't include this at the top of your CV. It states the obvious and just wastes space.

- Photo – remove this. In the UK, by including a photo, you reveal potential discrimination issues. It's illegal for employers to consider factors like age, race, gender, religion and national origin in hiring decisions. So prospective employers prefer to not 'officially' know whether you're a member of one of these protected classes. If you put a photo on your CV, you reveal some of these details. If the employer later interviews you but doesn't hire you, it opens the possibility of a discrimination claim. In extreme cases, some companies will even automatically reject CVs with photos, just to avoid that potential accusation. An exception to the rule would be if you were submitting a European CV, which fully supports photos.

- Address – you don't have to include your full address. Some people prefer not to, as if you post this online, you are opening yourself up to a security risk. An email address will suffice, along with your town and contact number.

- Email – keep it professional! You are a grafter, not a joker.

- Marital status/children/pets/non-smoker/driving licence – Why are these points relevant? No need to include! Only include non-smoker, driving licence if relevant to role.

- Don't include links to websites, videos etc, unless this is specified. Most employers print off CVs so they become irrelevant and it makes the CV look messy.

- Hobbies – only include if relevant. Again, some employers err on the side of caution. You may have a brilliant first class honours degree, but if you spend your weekends bungee jumping or carrying out other extreme sports it is best to leave this out. Employers may be concerned re injury; how much time would you have to take off due to an accident?

There is a lot of contradictory advice on the internet about how long a CV should be. Some say one page, most say 2-3. I would advise two in most cases, but it is all dependent on experience. Remember to check the application instructions. Some companies ask for a CV to be a certain number of pages, typed in a certain font.

Which brings me back to the layout. If you are sending a postal application, keep it simple. Remember, it is not a book you are sending for publication. Your CV doesn't need a front cover, content page and colour. This won't get you any further up in the pecking order, and will most likely irritate potential employers and will be put into the 'round file.' Same goes for binding it up –

don't! This will have to be picked apart for photocopying purposes and is an extra irritant.

3.2 Cover letter

A great cover letter should show enthusiasm and explain at a glance what you can bring to a role and the organisation. It should include your understanding and knowledge of the company and the skills that you have gained to be successful within the advertised position, along with the 'why?' criteria.

There are many different ways to write a cover letter, depending on your individual circumstances. These could include:

Graduate/first job – Is your degree relevant to the specific role? If not, you can still include work/study/undertaken, or research (for example, your dissertation) that may comply with your job = transferable skills. Pick a couple of points and expand on these. Remember to include any internships/placements/voluntary work/extra-curricular activities relevant to the role. Show ambition and your immediate availability to start work.

First job/school leaver – Highlight your motivation and passion for the role. Talk about your experiences at school, and mention the subjects you studied that will have the most impact on your application. Mention any hobbies/extra-curricular activities that may be relevant.

Unemployed – Don't be ashamed of unemployment; mention your work experience in an esteemed light, as you have done in the CV. This could be voluntary skills that you have undertaken, or a new skill you have learned since your last paid job. If you haven't achieved this, think of any hobbies, social activities or qualifications you have undertaken that could be transferred into this specific role. Turn your period of unemployment into a positive experience – it can give you time to reassess your options and think of what direction you want your career to go in.

Change of career – If you are applying for jobs in a completely different area, where you have no or little experience history in this particular field, you will need a strong cover letter to sell your strengths and skills. Think back to your education. Was there a specific element that would be relevant with this change? Be upfront about your career change, but don't bad mouth your previous companies, this shows unprofessionalism.

Career breaks – This could be a parent/carer returning to work, traveller or someone pursuing a personal or voluntary project. Whatever the reason, you can highlight your transferable skills for each specific role. For example, if you were raising a family you could emphasise your organisational and budgeting skills. If travelling, you could talk about your communication skills by meeting a diverse range of people. Working on a project would mean you gained skills in time management and planning. If you are moving back into a similar industry, mention your enthusiasm for the sector, and why you want to return to it. If you are targeting a different path, mention why you are ready for a new challenge.

Promotion/senior role – This should be one of the easiest letters to write. Not necessarily! There could be a lot of other candidates with the same skills as you, particularly if you are targeting an internal position, and others are well-known in the company. So you need to talk about specific achievements in terms of statistics. Explain what you have achieved most recently, and why you feel you are ready to take the next step to a higher level. Use your letter to highlight how long you have been in your current role, along with the skills and experience you have acquired.

And as with all job applications, take time to research the company and tailor your letter accordingly.

3.2 Application form

Nowadays it is also common practice for employers to ask you to fill out an application form; they won't even consider CVs. Why? They want to see if you can sell yourself, highlight your specific skills and give evidence of these. They don't want to be bombarded with lots of generic CVs. Also, serious applicants will only apply, as filling in an application form is more time-consuming than attaching a Word document to an email.

If prepared correctly, a good application form will take time to perfect. It needs to be tailored to a specific job specification, as well as essential and desirable criteria. But don't panic! This may seem like a daunting task, but once you have perfected it save it onto your computer, and you can then tweak it for future applications if you need to.

Application forms cover the same subjects as within a CV. You will need to list your qualifications and education history. Use the Profile and Key Skills, Knowledge and Expertise sections from your CV to fill in your supporting statement. The supporting statement within an application form is the most important part. Here, you will need to list all your relevant skills and experience in accordance with the company's job specification. Most companies will ask you to give evidence of your skills and experience in job specification order, to see if you meet the essential criteria. It is also important to fill this out for the desirable criteria too, to show you have a wide range of skills that would fit that role.

If you don't meet all the desirable criteria, don't worry. Do not make up stories just so you tick all the boxes! Remember, the information you put in your application will be used at interview and you will soon get found out if you have been dishonest. You are just wasting your and the company's time.

Some application forms are online, some you need to complete as a Word document and email this through. For some online applications, there is a word/character limit. If you go over your limit, you will not be able to send. So try and keep this as concise as possible, highlighting the essential criteria first. It shouldn't be too short or too long. It is tricky to get the balance right, but the more you do, the better you will get. The majority of companies follow the same format, so practice makes perfect.

What happens if you see a job you want to apply for but you don't meet all the essential criteria? Is it even worth applying? It depends on the criteria and the skills of the other applicants. Some job specifications are really specific, and some of the essential criteria can be demanding. You could get round this by saying, for example, 'although I don't have any experience working on databases within an [educational] environment, I have worked with several in-house databases and can learn new systems with ease.'

And remember, if you don't get shortlisted this time, don't be too disheartened. You are still gaining experience in application prep.

3.3 LinkedIn

Most people nowadays have some sort of online presence via social media. One such site, LinkedIn, is an extremely useful business marketing online tool. Used correctly, it can be a powerful way of keeping one step ahead of the competition in the market you are targeting. It can help to find and connect you with people. It can help to expand networks and find business opportunities. By creating an online marketing profile, you have now begun virtually networking.

Another benefit of LinkedIn is that you can gain endorsements from others, describing you as a person and what you are like to work with; a sort of online reference section. This is almost difficult to portray in a CV/cover letter and employers are keen to hire people that fit in well with the team, not just with the right experience and qualifications.

It is important that you create a positive first impression. Remember to be professional at all times and include a sensible photo. Having an unprofessional LinkedIn profile can portray you in a negative light, and can have a detrimental impact. A lot of employers nowadays use social media sites to find out more about prospective employees, so it pays to be professional.

So why include a photo here and not on a CV? This is because anti-discrimination laws are targeted towards job applications, which is what a CV is for. LinkedIn is effectively a networking site, where not everyone is looking for a job. Some join just to establish contacts and network. You're more likely to have your profile viewed if a photo is on. We are naturally a suspicious society, so people may think you have something to hide if a photo is not included. If you were looking for something on eBay, would you be more likely to bid for the item with a photo? Of course you would. It's the same for LinkedIn.

A regularly updated LinkedIn profile should include information about your skills and experiences. If you already have a CV prepared, take some information from the Profile and Key Skills sections, including achievements and examples of projects you have worked on.

The most important parts are the Summary and Experience sections. I prefer to write the summary in third person, as it looks like someone else is talking about you in glowing terms and a positive light. But whatever way suits you is fine, as long as the content is relevant.

You can include as much information as you want to within the summary, as long as it is no longer than 2,000 characters. But make it effective. Within the Skills section, include as many of your skills as you can; anything that can be justified for a future role. You can also add in any opportunities you are looking for.

Another benefit of using LinkedIn is that you can easily get involved in forums, groups and individuals in the same boat as yourself. This in itself can be an enormous support.

Large corporations are using LinkedIn more regularly to headhunt new talent. Even though you are not actively looking for a job, you never know when an unexpected opportunity may arise.

Chapter 4

The impact of social media on your career path

As discussed in section 3.4, most of our population uses some sort of social media, albeit for many different purposes, one of the most popular being Facebook and Twitter. Facebook can be an excellent source for networking also, although it is used on a more personal level than LinkedIn. I have found a few good freelancing jobs on Facebook, as this works by word of mouth. People are looking for someone with known credentials; maybe even an urgent job in a specific area. Within a few minutes you could have a list of ideal candidates, without having to spend a penny on advertising.

But posting on social media sites does have its disadvantages if done in a negative manner. How many times have you posted photos, or had an angry rant at somebody, only to immediately regret it? Too late, the damage has been done.

Prospective employers may look to your social media sites to try and gauge what sort of person you are before initial contact or interview. They want to see what makes you tick, to see if you would be a good fit for their business. Therefore, if you are serious about your ideal job/career, you need to make sure that there is no content that would have detrimental consequences on you successfully gaining employment. Pictures of drunken behaviour, abusive language, criminal offences or heated opinions will not bode well. Remember, if you over-share information, this may come back to haunt you.

Try angling your Facebook page towards a particular role, like you would a CV or application form. If you are volunteering to try and get into a certain market, post pictures and content regarding this. You could also start a blog and link this into your social media sites. As I mentioned in section 3.1, it is not advisable to add a link onto a CV, but with social media this would be a good way to show a prospective employer your key strengths in your chosen field. It shows you are proactive, enthusiastic and serious about your chosen career.

Remember, this is also the case in your current employment. Employers have been known to sack employees because of inappropriate content on social media sites. There goes your job, your reference, and will show a gap in your CV as well!

It is also advisable not to post negative comments regarding your current employer and fellow employees. It may feel therapeutic at the time, but bad-mouthing fellow employees shows a lack of maturity and could sometimes, if names are mentioned, breach confidentiality.

But before you go and hurriedly delete your profile, stop! If employers search for a prospective employee and find no information, this may be another disadvantage. Employers say that they are more likely to hire someone they find on social media that supported their job specification, qualifications and a wide range of interests, rather than someone with no online presence.

So, the golden rule is: if you can't say anything nice, don't comment on it!

Chapter 5

Interview skills and techniques

Congratulations! You've achieved your next career development stage and have secured an interview for your dream career. But once the elation dies down, you need to start preparing for that all-important meeting. I am now going to share with you some tips and techniques to help you on your way.

5.1 Types of interview

There are many different types of interview. These can consist of:

Face-to-face: Group, Panel, Individual, Informal chats
Virtual: Skype, Telephone

Sometimes you may be told in advance what format your interview is going to take, especially if there is more than one round to the interview process. Some larger companies start with an initial telephone interview, then, if you are successful, you will be put forward to a face-to-face second stage. However, you may not know until you arrive what the format will be. Therefore, you must be prepared for whatever is thrown at you.

Face-to-face interviews

With a face-to-face interview, body language is extremely important. You need to come across as impressionable, enthusiastic, confident and outgoing. And that's before you even start talking!

The Write Career recently conducted a survey. The one area that continually scored highly was personality, before industry knowledge and qualifications. Employers need to be able to see how well you would integrate as part of a team, and will be able to establish this relatively quickly. You may have the best qualifications and industry knowledge out of your peers, but if your face doesn't fit, then these may be deemed irrelevant. Harsh, but a reality.

Virtual interviews

These are probably the most difficult, because the interviewer and interviewee are not in the same room. Telephone interviews can be especially tricky, since both parties cannot see each other. The key to preparing for a telephone interview is to practise questions as you would for a face-to-face interview, but imagine you are presenting. Because interviewers cannot see your body language, your verbal communication methods must be enhanced, to ensure you come across as professional and enthusiastic. Therefore, you need to command a strong presence, be articulate and confident. Really over-emphasise your communication.

Practising presenting is a really effective way of doing this; stand up, walk around the room, use hand gestures. Of course, you obviously can't put these methods into practice when you are actually carrying out a virtual interview, but it will enable you to find your voice before your meeting. Prospective employers will then be able to determine your personality, skills, and if they think you will be an asset to their team.

You may think because prospective employers cannot see you, that it is acceptable to have your notes in front of you. This is not recommended. Employers can hear! A few pages rustling in the background is extremely off-putting, and gives the impression that you have not prepared. Which brings us onto the next stage – prep work.

5.2 Prep work

This may seem obvious, but do your homework beforehand. Nowadays it is easy to carry out research on any company. The disadvantage is that companies will expect you to look at their website. So a regurgitated verbatim statement lifted directly from their home page may not be deemed in the best light! It's better to go that extra mile to keep in front of your competitors, and find out information that isn't so easily shared. Some ways to do this are:

- Visit other websites that will provide different information.

- Seek information and development on market competitors.

- Research any special projects the company may have invested in.

- Find out if the company supports Corporate Social Responsibility, does it help a specific charity?

- Is there anyone you know that has had experience working for them, or developed business relations?

Venue

So, you know where the interview is being held. Are you sure? Remember to double check! A lot of companies have their HR department based in one location, which is where you would have sent your application to. This doesn't mean that the interview will be held there. There have been many occasions where interviewees were late because they hadn't checked the location properly.

If you are not sure where the venue is, it is advisable to do a 'dry run' if you can. If this is not possible, enter the details into your phone, and also print off a hard copy. It's amazing how many phones need recharged at the most inopportune times!

Check how long your journey will take and add on an extra 30-45 minutes. If you are driving, check for lane closures, delays and diversions. Public transport is totally outwith your control; trains and buses often run late due to unforeseen circumstances. It is better to be early than late; you can check your appearance, have a cup of tea to calm your nerves (nothing stronger until after the interview!) and have a last minute practise.

It is also advisable to have a contact phone number of the company (remember to print this off also). That way, if you are running late, you can call them to advise. This shows courtesy. It is not advisable to just rush in in a frenzy, babbling apologies. This is unprofessional.

Remember, employers are human! If you are late because of an unforeseen major traffic delay, they may try their best to accommodate you, if you call ahead beforehand.

5.3 Competency-based questions

Most interviews nowadays consist of competency-based questions which I mentioned in Chapter 3. To reiterate, competency-based questions are questions where you are asked to provide real examples and describe a situation where you demonstrated something in, like finishing a project, or using your initiative, or problem solving. By putting pointers of these in your CV or application form, you have already provided the basis for these answers. So make sure you revise what you have written, as the questions will be likely to be based on the scenarios you gave.

Remember to practise. And take a notebook and pen with you. Some questions have numerous stages to them. Some interviewers will advise you to write down the question so you do not forget the previous stages.

Some competency-based questions that you may be asked are:

• Tell me about your employment history.

• Why our company? What attracted you to this position?

• Give me an example of a time you worked in a team.

• What is your biggest achievement to date?

- What makes you different from the other candidates?
- Can you tell me about a time when you had to resolve an issue?
- Can you tell me about a time when you had to communicate a challenging piece of news?
- Describe a time when you had to work on your own initiative.
- Describe a time when you had to meet a strict deadline.
- What qualities do you think you have to succeed in this job?
- How would you cope with taking on an urgent task in the middle of your other duties?

These are examples that I have come across and are by no means exhaustive; you may be asked only a selection of these. To think of an answer, it is useful to break this down into stages, what is known as the STAR approach (Situation, Task, Action, Result). Describe the situation you were in, the task involved, what you did to complete the task, the result of the task, and the specific skills used. Remember also to highlight your achievements. Don't be shy, be proud! Now is the time to shine.

I've provided an example below to get you thinking. It doesn't have to be lengthy, just a simple scenario that you can describe in a methodical manner and that has a satisfactory conclusion.

'Describe a time when you had to meet a strict deadline and the difficulties that arose.'

Situation – One example would be in my current role as an admin assistant in a local accounts office, carrying out admin and finance-related skills.

Task – As part of my role, I have to ensure that all staff complete their timesheets by Friday, 5pm. This can be an extremely difficult task as sometimes I need to track down members of staff that are absent and manually fill in their timesheets for them, resulting in me not achieving a 100% capacity within timescale.

Action – I spoke with my line manager about this, and we implemented a monitoring process whereby I recorded incomplete timesheets for each week. If timesheets were not individually completed by the deadline, my manager explained to our team that because this could have a detrimental impact on the department's figures, disciplinary action would be taken against those individuals who failed to complete this task.

Result – I can now manage this more effectively and members of staff are more organised. This has resulted in our office having a 100% completion rate.

5.4 Dress to impress

How many times have we got ready for work, only to find out that the shirt we were going to wear is in the ironing basket? Or that a button is missing? Or that our shoes need cleaning? And how many of us actually take time to remedy these situations?

Most of the time, we don't! We leave just enough time in the morning to get up, wash, dress, breakfast (sadly, a lot of use see this as a luxury nowadays), and get to our place of work. If something interferes with this routine, we are inevitably late. We are in too much of a rush, so we just muddle through as best we can. No one will notice, will they?

But preparing for an interview is different. We need to impress, not just with the way we verbally present ourselves, but also in the physical way we present ourselves. Our dress sense says a lot about who we are. It is good to be unique and dress how we see is appropriate to our own nature. But we still need to fit into a certain category when targeting our interview audience. In the recent survey The Write Career carried out, employers stated that the way a prospective employee dressed was one of the other key things they looked for at interview. It shows that the employee has considered the position, dressed appropriately, and that they are keen to make a good impression and are motivated to do well.

What does dressing to impress mean? Simply, think of yourself as an interviewer. What would you expect from a candidate? The golden rule is to dress smart and professionally. The office you are going to may have a smart but casual rule, but still dress smart business for an interview.

- Clean, ironed shirt.

- Sensible tie, make sure top shirt button is closed.

- Dark socks (for men).

- Polished shoes.

- Clean trouser/skirt suit.

- Opaque or clear tights (check for ladders).

- Clean shoes, with a sensible heel length (the five inch black ones may look good, but if you can't walk properly this only gives you something else to worry about and you also may encounter problems sitting down/standing up).

- Make-up and jewellery – less is more! Go for the subtle approach.

Keep your hair neat secure off your face. This will give the interviewer a clearer impression of your expression, and you won't be tempted to play with it; this is a sign of nervousness.

Arrange clothes the night before and check from the list about for any potential mishaps. Iron, polish and sew. Forward planning is the key to a good interview. This will leave you with less stress the following morning, and you will feel confident knowing you have made an effort.

Remember to also dress appropriately for a virtual interview. You won't be seen (unless on Skype) but power dressing gives more motivation and provides a 'can-do' approach.

5.5   Body language

Social skills and body language also play an important part in the interview process, from the second we walk into the room.

Body language can tell us a lot about a person, for example, if they are confident, outgoing, withdrawn. It can take an interviewer as little as a few seconds to make up their mind about a candidate, so first impressions are extremely important. A firm handshake, eye contact throughout the interview, and a smile is a good way to engage the interest of your interviewer. If a group or panel interview, remember to make eye contact with everyone in the room, and not just focus on one specific person. If you appear relaxed and confident, it will put everyone at ease. Employers may be nervous too. Align your posture, don't slump. This will make you look lethargic.

It is a good idea to use gestures when in an interview, as this shows you are comfortable in your current surroundings. Symbolic gestures can help explain points and aid communication, for example, emphasising multiple points with your fingers. However, this doesn't come naturally to all. If you are a fidget, don't use them. You don't want to come across as an over-enthused octopus! Use your voice instead.

If you are prone to fidgeting, shaking, knee and leg wiggling, practise in front of a mirror. Or ask a friend to take you through a mock interview and film it. That way, you will be able to see for yourself your mannerisms and can change them accordingly.

Your voice is an extremely powerful tool. It shows others what you want to say, and how you want to say it. People can tell if you're happy, sad, angry, excited; and this is all down to tone. Without changing your pitch you sound monotone. This could be seen as boring, and the last thing you want to do is to put your interviewer to sleep.

Remember to project without shouting. Also, adapt your pace of talking. We naturally speed our speech up when we are nervous. Slowing your speech down will avoid the risk of sounding nervous and incoherent. Take pauses to draw breath and try and avoid 'verbal tics' such as 'um,' 'ah,' 'you know,' 'basically.' Always finish a sentence, don't just let your voice trail off into oblivion. This will only confuse the interviewer.

The way you exit an interview is just as important as the way you enter. Repeat the handshake, smile at everyone and thank them for their time. Leave a good lasting impression. Tip: if you are prone to sweaty hands, rub a little talc on before you leave for interview.

5.6 Ending the interview

We have all feared the dreaded saying 'any questions?' at some point in our interview histories. How many times have we practised questions to ask at the end of an interview, only to find out they have already been answered! What do you do? You have always been told to ask something! A good one is, if you are really stuck, is 'when can I expect to hear from you and what is the next stage?' A second interview may take place before any decisions are made, so it is good to know. Below are some questions you can ask if they haven't been already answered:

- How will the company help me develop?

- What are the most important objectives of this position?

- Can you tell me how the role relates to the overall structure of the organisation?

- How would you describe the work culture?

- How is performance measured and reviewed?

- If I do get the job, when would you like me to start?

I think it is also productive to send a thank you email the day after your interview. 'Why?' I hear you ask. 'Is that not a little bit sycophantic?' Picture this: you gave an excellent interview, clicked with the interviewers and made it known you were keen on the job. But did you? Sometimes, it is better to put this in writing; give hard evidence that you would be delighted to commence work with this company. It doesn't have to be long and rambling, just enough to register your interest and keep your name fresh in the heads of those who interviewed you. Something along the lines of:

'*Dear [name]*

Thank you for meeting with me thismorning/afternoonto discuss the [Office Administrator] position. I enjoyed our conversation, and I am very excited about the possibility of joining your team.

The job seems to be an excellent match for my skills and interests. I appreciate the time you took to interview me and Iam very interested in working for you and look forward to hearing from you regarding this position in due course.

Best wishes

[name]'

Now imagine that the interviewer thought you would be a great fit within their team. But they are struggling to decide between you and one other person. And imagine if you were the only one that took the time to contact them and express your interest. Which person would you choose? The one that showed initiative and courtesy, or the one that kept silent? A quick, four sentence email may be all that stands between you and your dream job.

Chapter 6

Work in progress

6.1 No room for complacency

You have prepared your mind map, decided what role you want to target, tailored your CV to suit, gave an outstanding interview, and you have now landed your dream job. Your classic career. Congratulations! The End. Without meaning to sound clichéd, you can rest on your laurels now, can't you? Well, this may not be the case. Your career could have a happy ending at this stage, or further down the line you may decide this isn't for you after all. Just because you have achieved what you set out to do, doesn't mean that's it. People's interests and priorities change; you may have decided to give up full-time work for part-time, or are targeting another industry after having a family. Team dynamics also change, and you may find your classic career has taken an unexpected twist. Whatever the reason, you will need to put into practice the same steps as you did to develop your classic career the first time round. Makes sense, doesn't it?

It is sometimes difficult to decide to start afresh. A useful tool that I have found extremely helpful, both with business and personal goals, is to carry out a SWOT analysis (Strengths, Weaknesses, Opportunities and Threats).

The purpose of the SWOT analysis is to identify actions you can take to meet the requirements of a specific job you are pursuing. Comparing your strengths, weaknesses, opportunities and threats will identify areas you need to work on, and will help you prepare to be the best candidate for the position. Divide a sheet of paper into four sections, and name each section as above. Then list all your SWOT items under each section.

I'll give you a case study as an example. Peter is an excellent project manager. He can liaise effectively and authentically within the small teams he manages. He knows how to lead these teams to get results, and has successfully delivered on each project he has managed, within budget and ahead of timescale.

Having been in the same role for a number of years, he is looking for a new challenge, and has heard of an internal promotion for which he would like to apply for as senior project manager for a large department. Although Peter has excellent skills as shown above, his ability to communicate with large groups of people lets him down and he thinks he may be out of his depth. He doesn't know if he should apply for this job, or stay where he is and try to be content that he has climbed to the top of his scale.

Peter's SWOT could consist of the following:

STRENGTHS
Project management skills.
Strong leadership of small teams.
Successful sales abilities.
Authentic communicator.
Achieves targets.

WEAKNESSES
Public speaking to large audiences.
Doubt in ability to
progress to next level.
Difficult to sell own skills.

OPPORTUNITIES
Enrol on a presentation
coaching skills course.
Speak to manager about
promotion/training prospects.
Go on a secondment to gain
experience and see if this job is for me.

THREATS
Career development may be hindered.
Team may progress before
me due to my fears.
Peers are more qualified
than me/better at speaking large groups.

See your weaknesses as an area of opportunity for growth, threats as goals to turn into opportunities and you strengths as your selling skills.

By compiling your SWOT, you'll be amazed at what you can find out about yourself, and you will also have a solid goal to work towards. It is interesting to revisit your SWOT analysis every so often. You will find you can change things around, sometimes weaknesses become strengths, and/or opportunities.

Having a solid plan you can refer back to will help you to come to a decision by taking all aspects into account.

6.2 Regular CV updates

You'd be surprised at how many CVs I've seen that are not up to date. There's been many a time when I thought a person's employment history ended in 2012. 'No,' I'm told when I enquire further, 'I just forgot to add in my current position.' This is a faux pas on two occasions 1) It looks like you have not been in employment for the last three years and 2) It shows that you can't be bothered to take the time to update your CV.

Imagine if you were searching for a service on the internet and you come across two websites that fit your remit. Now, one website is current and states when it was last updated. The second, however, still has a big banner on the front page saying 'The Big Sale – not to be missed! Ends 2 May 2013.' Which one would you give your business to? If the front page was wrong, what are the chances of the prices being wrong too? Everything about the first example screams inactivity.

The same can be said for your CV. And it's not just the present we have to update, it's also the past. As we get older, we obviously gain more experience as we climb the career ladder. We try new things, move companies and aim for higher-level roles. The same rules apply as I mentioned in Chapter 3; keep your CV relevant and simple. This means you don't have to state all the roles you have had since 1984. This will take up needless amounts of paper and will contain too much information for an employer to read.

Be ruthless, as you would editing a book, and have a spring clean. You'll be amazed at how good it feels!

Also remember to update your qualifications and training, along with your key skills, knowledge and expertise. You may find, for example, that you have gained leadership experience since your last update, which is another 'buzzword' which can be added in this section.

Regularly updating your CV whilst tracking your recent accomplishments, awards and achievements will make it easier for you to respond to last minute job opportunities, keep your mind fresh and help you to revisit why you are looking for a new job in the first place; refocus on your career and prepare that all-important SWOT. It is vital to your career development and creating your classic career.

6.3 Negotiation skills

Once you reach your goal, complacency will set in after a while. This is only natural. But as mentioned previously, your classic career goalposts can change. Personal and professional dynamics alter throughout our working life, which could mean what you once thought was your ultimate goal is no more. But what if you are happy with the company you work for, and your job for that matter, but you sense that something is missing? Maybe you feel that you have been given too much responsibility for the role you have, and you feel you deserve a financial reward? Or, maybe you feel you need *more* responsibility in the company.

Whatever, the reason, don't let your feelings fester. Don't start complaining to all in sundry about how fed-up you feel. You will then be in danger of letting this situation snowball out of control until you are known as the office moaning minnie. It's better to be authentic; speak to your manager about how you feel. I did this in an early role, and I found it hugely beneficial. Not only did we set out concise goals about my future role in the company, but I also managed to secure an unexpected pay rise, and felt more valued as a member of the team (it should be worth noting that a pay rise isn't guaranteed!).

However, negotiating effectively is a delicate process, and should be thought about and timed carefully. One wrong word could make or break the situation.

There are many stages in the negotiation process, namely:

- Preparation before the meeting

- Discussion

- Goal setting and clarification

- Negotiate a win-win situation

- Implement an action plan with set timescales

With these in mind, why not try and prepare a mind map to help your situation? This could be along the lines of:

Negotation mind map

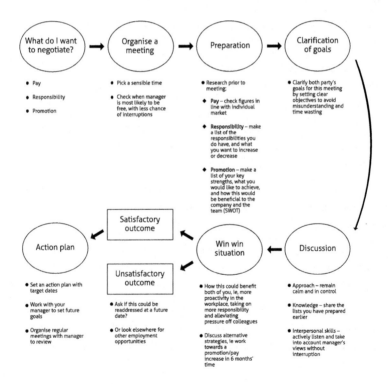

Sometimes, once you have prepared your mind map and having undertaken thorough research, you may realise there might not be an opportunity to negotiate at this present time, so it always useful to plan before you go charging in.

Try and pick a time when your manager is free to talk. Check their diaries and ask for a meeting. Don't just flag them down in the canteen, corridor or car park. It is probably best to avoid Monday mornings and Friday afternoons, as these are the times when staff are most busy/preoccupied. Tell them you wish to speak to them about your job strategies. Any manager worth their salt will be pleased you have shown initiative to have a chat.

It's also best not to start with 'I want a pay increase/promotion.' Take time to prepare for your meeting. Write down what you want to say, and how you are going to say it. Remember when I mentioned body language in Chapter 5? This is an important part of any negotiation technique. The way you use your voice and mannerisms will be instrumental to the outcome of this meeting.

Approach

Depending on the circumstances, this may be a very emotional meeting for you. But try and keep your emotions in check. Shouting and screaming if you don't get your own way will do you no favours whatsoever. Show your maturity by speaking in a slow, concise manner, backing up your presentation with some facts and figures.

Knowledge

Good preparation is essential; if you are in control of the facts and figures you have prepared you will have a stronger case to negotiate. It will also show your manager that this isn't a whim, you have shown in detail what you want to achieve, and how you want to achieve it.

Interpersonal skills

It is extremely important to listen to what the other party is saying throughout any negotiation meeting. This means not cutting off the other person's sentences either. You will be understandably nervous, but take time to listen objectively to your manager's views. You will have played this scenario out in your head lots of times, but unfortunately no one can predict what the outcome will be. So don't hear what you *want* to hear; actively listen and you will find this is a much more effective way of dealing with the situation.

Remember to be open-minded about the outcome. Sometimes there may not be an opportunity at this stage for your end goal. You will then have to decide if this is something you can work towards, or it may be the time to look for alternative employment with a company who can give you what you are looking for.

Chapter 7

Change your life

We've all been there. Even when we have secured our perfect job, we still have our own little mind monkeys constantly confusing us. Fear of success, fear of failure, fear of not being good enough, fear of starting again. Sound familiar? Well, you'll be pleased to know that fear is normal. We need fear. Fear pushes us forward. It challenges us and inspires us to take action. Addressing and recognising fear is an important part of your career development. It is vital to embrace fear in order to gain success.

7.1 Career fears

How many of us have applied for jobs, secured an interview and immediately gone down the 'what if?' route. 'What if I don't get it?' 'What if I can't answer the questions?' 'What if they don't like me?'

'What ifs' create a negative energy. It is pointless to worry about things you can't control. Worrying constantly about 'what ifs' can be mentally exhausting. In order to minimise these thoughts, try and distract yourself from worry. Give yourself a 'window' each day when you are allowed to think about your 'what ifs.' Then, imagine you have put all those worries into a bucket. Now, tie the bucket to a balloon and watch your worries float off, away from you.

This may take some practise, but the more you try the more effective it will become. Another useful tool is to put an elastic or hair band around your wrist. Every time you feel a 'what if' coming on, ping the band. Not only will it hurt, but it will have reminded you to stop thinking in this manner. Accept what you can't change. You can't control a person's thoughts, behaviours or actions. So it is pointless thinking about it. What you *can* do is change the way you handle a potentially negative situation and turn it into a positive one. This is known as reframing – plan a strategy for worries you *can* control.

Ok, so, imagine you have just come out of an interview for a role you have been seeking for some time. You are feeling energised and positive. It went well. Then, as the day wears on, you start to overthink things. You realise there was something you didn't mention that you should have. You start to doubt yourself, maybe you weren't as good as you thought? Your little mind monkeys start to creep in and take over with negativity.

STOP! The interview is over, and there is nothing you can do about it now. Hindsight is a wonderful thing. This is the point when your reframing/planning can be put into force – what have you gained from this experience?

Let's look at the following table for some specific examples of how reframing can put things into perspective:

Action	Old thought	New thought (reframing)
No response after job application.	Why me? That shows lack of courtesy.	I tried my best. Maybe I need to go back and revisit my application to see how I can make it better? Maybe the job wouldn't have been right for me anyway?
Rejection after interview.	It's not fair, I got so close.	I have gained interview experience. They must have liked my CV/job application for me to have got to interview process in the first place. So I am doing something right. I will ask for feedback so I can work on my interview technique.
Unsatisfactory outcome after promotion negotiations.	Typical, my manager hasn't encouraged me from the start. Why should I bother? I should just go back to doing the bare minimum.	I managed to negotiate, albeit the outcome wasn't what I expected. The next time will be better. I will ask my manager what I need to do to gain promotion, and ask if I am suitable. If not, I will rethink my career prospects with this company.

Be kind to yourself. Challenging your assumptions whilst acknowledging the positive with the negative will enable you to move forward more quickly, and gain that career that you so richly deserve.

7.2 Breaking from the old routine

You know the old story, you begin a job to get your foot onto the career ladder, and before you know it 20 years have passed and you are no further forward. That's why all the techniques I have shared with you in previous chapters are so important. It keeps you on track and reminds you of your action plans.

Career breaks are also extremely helpful in reframing your mind to help you to decide what you want to do. By this, I mean taking time out to actually do something positive; volunteer with a charity overseas, or help a local community project. This doesn't mean going to Spain for 6 months, sunbathing and drinking. Sometimes it is good to get away from everyday living, it can help you reassess your life, what is important to you, and enable you to develop new skills.

I'll give you an example. We'll call him Joe. Joe loved motorbikes and he always dreamed of opening his own workshop, fixing Harley Davidsons. One of his ambitions was train with Harley Davidson in Milwaukee. So he took a six month sabbatical, went to America, and fulfilled his dream. Now, he could have stayed, but he didn't. He had realised his dream was just a hobby. He didn't want it as a full-time career. And that's the beauty of taking time out to reframe and re-evaluate what we want. Sometimes, things aren't the same in real life as they are in our heads. Joe also developed new skills that he could put on his CV. And he actually got a new job when he returned, within the same company, but it meant worldwide travel. The reason he was successful? His sabbatical showed that he wasn't afraid to travel to new places. So, although he didn't get the job he *thought* he wanted he ended up with the right one in the end. Its funny how things work out, isn't it?

Chapter 8
Summary and contacts

Now is the time to end my guide to creating your classic career. Below is a glance-at-guide to everything that has been discussed in my book, which you can refer back to should you require. I've also added some contacts at the end that I think you will find useful, along with a glossary of key terms and real life case studies to motivate you on your journey.

I hope I have provided you with a passion to go on and find out what stimulates you. Maybe after reading this, you've realised you are in the right vocation after all. Self-discovery is great, although as this book suggests, it has to be worked at to arrive at the correct conclusion.

On a final note; it's up to you to change your future. No one else can do that for you. Good luck!

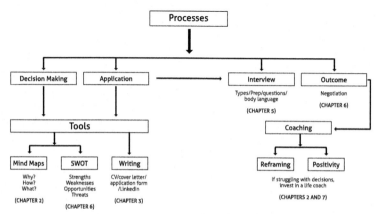

Glossary

Buzzwords – Positive words that make your CV stand out, including: Teamwork, Leadership, Communication Problem Solving, Negotiation, Customer service, Dedication.

Competency-based questions – Interview questions aimed at providing real-life answers to particular scenarios.

CV structure – Profile, Key Skills, Knowledge & Expertise, Employment History, Education and Qualifications.

Interviews – Face-to-face: Group, Panel, Individual, Informal chats Virtual: Skype, Telephone

Mind map – Used to visually organise thought processes and information.

Negotiation – Discussions aimed at reaching an agreement that all parties are happy with.

Reframing – Turning negative events, feelings and experiences into a positive light.

SMART goals – Specific, Measurable, Attainable, Realistic, Time-bound. Used to summarise performance expectations.

STAR – Situation, Task, Action, Result – a methodical process used in interview skills to answer competency-based questions.

SWOT analysis – Used to find out your key Strengths, Weaknesses, Opportunities, Threats. Can be used on a personal or a professional level.

For more information

Alison Spencer
Career Development Consultant
The Write Career
07986 110 566
www.write-career.com
Links to blogs and advice, subscription to newsletter
www.facebook.com/writecareer
Updates and career information

Leila Khan
Life Is Today Academy
0141 582 1268
info@lifeistodayacademy.com
www.lifeistodayacademy.com
Twitter & IG: @lklifeistoday
Facebook: Life Is Today Academy
Author | Life Mastery and Leadership Expert | Speaker | Teacher | Mentor

Moraig Hewitt Creative Textiles
mhcreativetextiles@gmail.com

Appendix – Real-life case studies

Case study one

Mags started out working as a secretary within the recruitment and defence sectors. She is now an Advocacy Worker. Here is her story …

1. **Can you tell me about your career ambitions when you left school? What is it that you wanted to become/achieve?**

   I didn't really know to be honest. I just enjoyed administration and business so thought I would like to do that at college. I didn't have a career goal at that point.

2. **How long were you in this career for? What changes in circumstance made you think that this wasn't for you?**

   11 years. In my mind I had been looking to do something that was more people-focused as I wanted to help others and to feel that my skills could help someone.

3. **How did you reach your current career goal? What plans/ strategies did you put in place to achieve this?**

   I contacted college to find out about study. I applied for HNC Social Care and did not get onto the course straight away, feedback was to get some voluntary work experience. I did that and I was accepted onto the course the following year. I was then working full-time, volunteering one night a week (and later on a placement at the weekend too). I then got my first job, and I was in that a year and a few months, next job five years. I had my sights set on being an advocacy worker, so I did more volunteering work and studied counselling skills. I now have a job I love! It's got all my skills rolled in together in it.

4. How difficult was it to achieve this goal and what struggles (if any) did you face?

Time factor was a struggle, balancing everything and there was little time for socialising, however in my mind I knew it wasn't for ever.

5. How has developing a complete career change impacted on your life? How do you feel now?

I feel proud of myself for my dedication and commitment to making the change and I know I could do it again if I had to.

6. What advice would you give to someone struggling in their current role?

Work out the skills you have, what you enjoy doing, then sign up to job sites to see what jobs come up that require your skills to help you decide if you need something completely different or a different job in the same field.

Case study two

Moraig left school at 17 to work in a travel agency, before going to university to gain her qualification in dietetics and then working as a dietician within the NHS. She now runs her own textile business, Moraig Hewitt Creative Textiles, along with teaching sewing workshops. Here is her story ...

1. **Can you tell me about your career ambitions when you left school? What is it that you wanted to become/achieve?**

   I didn't have any. I was terrified of leaving the safety of school and stayed to the end of Sixth Year. I knew a tertiary education wasn't going to suit me at that time and I had no great self-awareness at the age of 17 to know where to start looking for a career or even what might suit me. I did have two part-time jobs that fitted around school and I knew I liked working with people (customers), but that was about it. I didn't feel academic, which was how I perceived all of my fellow sixth year pupils, but when I did try for full-time jobs in retail, I was turned down at the end of interviews, being told I was over-qualified and therefore unlikely to stay. In reality, I just wanted to leap from the safety of an institution to a stable job, without another four years of study.

2. **How did you achieve this? (Please give examples of study, etc). If you didn't achieve this, where did you end up?**

   I had to find a job after leaving school and the local careers service helped me secure interviews for YTS positions at two travel agencies, plus one at the headquarters of an insurance group. The two travel agency interviews were first and I was offered a job which I took. I turned down the interview for the insurance company, perceiving it to be monotonous office work, compared to albeit a lower paid job, but with the potential for every day to be different, as well as dealing with people.

3. How long were you in this career for? What changes in circumstance made you think that this wasn't for you?

I stayed with the travel agency for four years. After four years, I had a chance conversation with someone I'd been to school with who was loving university and it made me wonder whether it could be something I could do. I'd already started to find work less stimulating and had spent a year at night school to get my Higher Modern Studies certificate and had looked at changing jobs. I got a copy of several university prospectuses and started to look for a course that looked interesting, knowing that I'd happily go to night school for another year to top up any qualifications I needed. I chose a vocational degree course that needed me to improve my Higher Chemistry grade and refresh my maths skills, but would hopefully lead to a job quickly after graduating. In the end, I had a job three months before I was due to sit my university finals, so was extremely lucky. I stayed in that career for eight years, working my way up to the position of Senior Renal Dietitian, within a busy inner city NHS trust.

I left this career when I was on maternity leave with my first child as my husband's job moved us 40 miles away, which was too far a commute with no suitable local childcare in our area that would allow me to continue working. I spent the next eight years raising our family as an at home mum. Dietitians and other health care professionals such as physiotherapists are not allowed to return to work after two years' absence without a significant amount of retraining and professional revalidation at the individual's expense. This was going to be difficult in the very rural area we live in, plus with the limited childcare available, and our stretched, single income, it became an insurmountable problem.

4. How did you reach your current career goal? What plans/ strategies did you put in place to achieve this?

Because we were losing a third of our household income as soon as I started maternity leave and had to move house, we started making economies in every area of our budget. I bought a sewing machine, with the thought of being able to make curtains and blinds to save money. After a few years and various soft furnishings later, I saw an adult education sewing course in our local town and enrolled on it, keen to learn new techniques and expand my repertoire. I became hooked, loving every new technique we were taught. After two years, the adult classes were closing, but the tutor was a City and Guilds tutor who taught the course at the weekends, once a month for two years. This fitted in with our family situation and I completed the course in 2014. Despite friends and family asking what I was going to do with my new qualification, I wanted to take things as they came. I'd started working in a fabric and craft shop part-time and was continuing to learn and develop at a textile art masterclass.

5. How difficult was it to achieve this goal and what struggles (if any) did you face?

The initial career change was barely a struggle, more a four year adventure that the 17 year old me would have thought impossible. The biggest struggle was going on my final placement. It was for nine months, in a large town, in a different country, almost 400 miles away from where I lived. I knew no one, was in grotty accommodation on my own, doing an unpaid, full-time job. It sounds clichéd, but it didn't occur to me at any point to give up. I fell back on all my previous work experience, walked into a nice looking local pub and started working in the evenings and at weekends, which gave me some cash, and more importantly, a social life that didn't cost me money.

Giving up my second, postgraduate job didn't seem difficult at first, in fact, because of the way health professionals are treated when they have stopped work for a period of two years or more, going back seemed harder. And more expensive. And more of a logistical nightmare than anything I'd done before. Having said that, after eight years of not working, it was becoming more and more difficult to feel any self-worth. Going to the adult education class five years ago was one of those fortuitous events that has now led to my new, fledgling career as a self-employed textile artist.

6. **How has developing a complete career change impacted on your life? How do you feel now?**

Going back to studying was great. I had to find the space in my head to work and concentrate, shutting out at home mum niggles for a few hours. When I gave up dietetics, I think I always knew I was unlikely to return to the NHS and didn't want to start a private practice. These days, I have a workroom at home, where I aim to work 10-3 at least three days a week, plus I work one day a week in the fabric shop and occasionally teach workshops, which is an area of my work I am keen to expand. This means I can take the kids to school, pick them up and be available to take them to any after school events. I can work extra hours at weekends or during the evenings, which also means I don't have to stop working completely during the school holidays. As soon as I started to work part-time, my self-worth started to return. I sometimes feel a bit sad that I gained a degree and postgraduate career and no longer use it, but remind myself that on top of the academic knowledge, I had gained transferable skills and a lot of valuable experiences during those 12 years that I wouldn't necessarily have if I hadn't taken the same forks in the paths that I did.

7. **What advice would you give to someone struggling in their current role?**

Think about the skills you have, which ones are transferable? What do you enjoy in your role? What don't you enjoy? Are the aspects you find enjoyable something you might want to expand, or develop into a new area? Use your weekends and spare time to explore hobbies, subjects or jobs that you feel an affinity to. Be open minded to possibilities – whatever is on offer might not be the perfect solution to your problem, but it might just lead you there.

Case study three

Graham started out working as a Lab Technician due to his love of science. He now works for a global bank as a Technical Specialist. Here is his story ...

1. **Can you tell me about your career ambitions when you left school? What is it that you wanted to become/achieve?**

   I had no clear career ambitions when I left school and really just went with what I enjoyed at school which was science.

2. **How did you achieve this? (Please give examples of study, etc). If you didn't achieve this, where did you end up?**

   As I had failed my Highers I went full-time to college for a year and to retake Highers and obtain a City & Guilds qualification. That got me a job as a Lab Technician and employment with day release at college to do my ONC, HNC etc.

3. **How long were you in this career for? What changes in circumstance made you think that this wasn't for you?**

   In different companies and roles for 19 years. I had started to get interested in IT and there was a lack of career progression in the lab work. The company I was working with was starting to scale-back investment in research.

4. **How did you reach your current career goal? What plans/strategies did you put in place to achieve this?**

   I went back to college to get an HNC in Computing and then university to gain a degree.

   I also took up any IT tasks in my current role and looked to move into an IT role within the same company.

5. **How difficult was it to achieve this goal and what struggles (if any) did you face?**

   It took a lot longer than I thought and required a fair amount of study in my own time. The hardest thing was getting the first job and convincing people that I could change career.

6. How has developing a complete career change impacted on your life? How do you feel now?

I enjoy my job much more now and it keeps providing new challenges.

7. What advice would you give to someone struggling in their current role?

Go for it but it may take longer than you think and you will need to do a fair amount of work yourself.

Author's Biography

Alison Spencer is a Career Development Consultant and runs her own business, The Write Career. She started off working in recruitment in 1994 and has had various jobs within recruitment and the financial sector. It was while she was having a particularly bad time at work that she realised she didn't have to be in a job  she hated. She took time out to discover and visualise what it was she wanted to do, and that was when The Write Career was born.

Alison has had a lot of success in helping clients gain employment through helping them to create and develop their passion into a dream career. She has also written a column for her local newspaper on career advice and has written and developed several workshops for schools and professionals. She lives near Glasgow with her husband and two children.

Lightning Source UK Ltd.
Milton Keynes UK
UKOW05f0849270117
293017UK00015B/225/P